Surviving the Boss From Hell:

Taming Tyrants, Soothing Screamers, and Outsmarting Control Freaks

Ken Williams

ISBN: 9798394028366

DEDICATION

To the difficult managers I've ever known who have made
this book possible.

And to the peers and friends I've had who have made this
book necessary.

If you're wondering whether you are one or the other…I
have no comment.

CONTENTS

ACKNOWLEDGMENTS

I didn't realize how helpful having a life coach was until I became one.

This book is the product of many coaches I've had throughout the years. Formal coaches, informal coaches. Paid coaches, and volunteer coaches. Coaches who didn't realize what they were doing, and coaches who knew *exactly* what they were doing.
So, in no particular order, Mom, Marcene, Gabrielle, Ron, Mark, Annette, and many others I surely have forgotten.

Thank you. I'm a better person for being coached by you.

AN INTRODUCTION:

THE "BOSS FROM HELL" DILEMMA

First of all, let me be clear. VERY clear.

I am not talking about *anyone* in particular. If you know me personally or have heard my podcast, the "Bad Boss Podcast" (And seriously, you should go listen to it. Not right now—I don't want to interrupt the momentum you are gaining by reading this book, but before the end of the day, look for it in your favorite podcast app. It's everywhere.) you may be thinking you know who I'm talking about as I share my brilliance and insights.

False.

I am not talking about him. Or her. I'm not talking about any single individual that I currently work with or have ever worked with in the past. I'm talking about someone else.

The stories I share are probably embellished and exaggerated for the purpose of entertainment and instruction. Conversations were invented. Situations were contrived. They are imaginary. At least as far as you know.

Now, having said that, you probably know people who are like the ones I will be describing. As far as you are concerned, THEY are the people I'm talking about. But just generally. Because there is also a very real chance that the people you know are the same people I have worked with and for in the past. That is simply coincidence. A happy little accident. I did that on purpose so that my stories seem more real to you.

Enjoy the overlap. Be amused with the convenient juxtapositions. But don't for a second believe that it was intentional in any way.

I have a great relationship with my boss. (Truly!) I have learned a lot from him and by working with him.

My purpose in writing this book is simple. There are a LOT of bad bosses out there. I've heard the stories. I might have even seen evidence of them. There's plenty of story fodder for a book like this.

However, I learned something recently. Now, for context, I'm a certified life coach. I love what I do, and one of the things I have discovered is that I can't change anyone other than me.

Honestly, it didn't take becoming a life coach to figure that one out. I've been married for 33 years (in a row!) to the same woman. I have five kids. I grew up as the oldest of six. I have had a LOT of experience NOT being able to change anyone else.

At the same time, I was frustrated that everyone else couldn't see that MY way was the best way to be. Coaching helped me frame that a little bit. So, as you read this book, expect to be coached a little. Hopefully you'll be slightly entertained, as well. And you can't change the boss from Hell to become the amazing boss that *I* am…but you <u>can</u> change you.

So, let's play with that for a minute. Let me give you a summary of the coaching model that I use. There are five parts: Circumstances, Thoughts, Feelings, Actions, and

Results. **Circumstances** are the facts that EVERYONE would agree on. **Thoughts** are what you think about the circumstance. **Feelings** come from the thoughts you have. Our feelings drive our **Actions** and give us **Results**.

I'm going to keep this light for now, but there are three things I need us to agree on.

First, circumstances are neutral. Not good, not bad. We can argue about this later, but trust me. "It's raining outside" is a fact. Neutral, We both agree (if, in fact, it is raining.)
"It's a crappy weather day" is a thought. I may hate the rain, and you may love the rain, so we aren't going to agree that it's a crappy weather day.

Just like "My boss is a narcissist." Unless she is diagnosed as a narcissist by a clinical expert, that is a thought—not a fact.

Number two: Thoughts are subjective, and they drive our feelings. Good thoughts bring good feelings. Bad thoughts bring bad feelings. We can choose our thoughts. This is where we get our power. We can talk more about this later.

Finally, our actions—our behaviors—*come from our FEELINGS*. How we feel (or think we will feel) creates our actions. Understand your thoughts and feelings, and you can control the actions and results you get.

It is not always necessary (or practical) to change the circumstance (your job is a circumstance. Your boss is also a circumstance.) You can get tangible change by thinking a bit differently. Still, maybe it's best for you to move on to another boss. That's a real option. But in the meantime, let's talk about how you can survive the Boss from Hell.

CHAPTER ONE

DECODING THE DIFFICULT BOSS:
TYRANT TO TIME WASTER

There are a lot of different types of bosses. And they all have different reasons for being the way that they are. And from the outside, the reasons all suck, and the ways are all stupid. I agree. I am one of those bosses sometimes. My reasons suck. They don't make sense all the time, and the way I manage is sometimes stupid.

Let's address some different styles.

I have been around a LOT of people who are new in leadership positions. Taking off a regular t-shirt and replacing it with a shirt that reads "leader" on the back is a very simple (and sometimes literal) way that some people dip their toe into leadership. (And I understand that "leadership" is not the same as "management," but stick with me here. For my own personal convenience, I'm going to use those terms somewhat interchangeably.)

So yesterday, they weren't a leader. Then some paperwork happened, and now they are magically a leader. We are supposed to follow them.

There's often no formal training. Some people have natural talent, and lots of people don't. Right? We've noticed that over the years.

When I promoted to my current management position, I wasn't sure how it would all work. I was afraid that my team might not follow me. And even worse, I was afraid that they *might.*

I don't think I was unique in that experience. Changing identity from being a non-leader to a leader takes time. It doesn't normally happen overnight.

So, I've noticed a lot of recently promoted people (and even some not-so-recently promoted people) compensate for the incongruous identity by using volume. If they speak louder (that means "yell") they imagine—or at least hope—they can get results.

I was shocked the first time I stepped into a leadership role and people wanted to hear what I had to say *simply because* I was in that role.

As soon as the word on the back of your shirt says "leader," you will automatically and instantly have some level of respect. Frankly, that may just be "positional" respect—we may not like the President, but we probably have some level of respect for the position that he or she holds…make sense?

Positional respect happens automatically. The rest—the earned respect that we can add to our style, comes with time. I think it grows with us along with our identity.

So, imagine a newly promoted leader who feels some level of imposter syndrome. They may compensate by yelling. Or demanding. Or requiring. Or Compelling.

What if that's simply a by-product of an incongruity between their identity and their job title?

And that's not the only thing that can happen with a leader. It's true that some of them are power-grabbing jerks. They like telling people to do things simply because they can. They might be lazy or sadistic. Maybe their mother didn't love them. Who knows?

Some bosses are delegators. They don't do anything that they don't have to do themselves. I know one of these. I've watched him rise through the ranks, and he would hand off *everything* that he could to anyone who would take it.

And then there's the micromanager. The one who not only tells you *what* to do, but also *how* to do it. Because your failure is a reflection of them.

I'm sure I haven't covered every possible scenario. Who has time for that?

So, how do you deal with that? Start with respecting the position.

They are in that position because someone saw something in them that they thought was worthy of the person becoming a leader of people. You maybe don't see the same thing. And bad news: that doesn't matter. You weren't the decision maker. Neither was I. So, we get to live with the consequences of someone else's judgment.

It's very tempting to complain about the difficult boss—and I'm not saying you shouldn't. I am saying, however, that I think you should slow down. Diagnose the problem. What *really* is bothering you. Give it a name. Is your boss a tyrant? A bully? A micromanager? A yes-man or yes-woman? A doormat?

Something interesting about people's actions: There is a reason for them. One hundred percent of the time, people have a reason for doing the things they do. (That reason may not be rational—or even conscious—but it exists nonetheless.

Imagine that you could discern the reason. Maybe they were dropped on their head when they were eleven. Maybe they don't have friends. Maybe they were falsely accused of having a personality. Whatever the reason, if you knew it, you would have a better understanding of the *why* behind the behavior or the management style.

Spend a few minutes with the Boss. Ask questions. What motivates them? What are their pet peeves? Why are they the way that they are?

The reason itself doesn't necessarily matter, and you don't have to agree with it. But understand, that their reason makes them them. Maybe they'll change, and maybe they won't. But knowing what you can expect from them will get you started in your own personal journey of not hating your job so much.

Now, don't think that I am defending their poor behavior. I am not. I don't like bullies. I don't think they should be promoted. But unfortunately, they are. And sometimes they are promoted to be your boss.

So, respect the position. And figure out why she is behaving the way she is. Discuss with a trusted friend, spouse, or coach. (Even with me, if you want. I'd be happy to share my perspective.) As you understand your boss a little better (again, I'm not saying you should agree with or condone bad behavior, but understand it.) you will be miles ahead of your peers in being able to work with the Boss from Hell.

CHAPTER TWO

STRATEGIC BROWN-NOSING:
MAKING YOUR BOSS BELIEVE
THEY'RE YOUR FAVORITE PERSON

Writing this book makes me a little bit uncomfortable. Because if you know and work with me, you are going to learn some of my secrets. So, I ask you to use this information wisely.

Again, I'm not talking about who you think I'm talking about. Fair enough?

Several years ago, I was asked to teach an early morning bible study class for high school students. We met for about 45 minutes before school. The kids were great, and I had an amazing experience.

I wanted them each to have an amazing experience as well, and I remember realizing that when I personally liked an instructor, I tended to listen more intently to him or her.

I decided that I could become the teacher that people liked. And the ideal way to do that was to let each of my students *believe* that he or she was my favorite.

Now, I have had a variety of experiences with this general concept, and I'll shortcut my education for you here. Basic lessons:

1. I have a LOT of favorites. And having multiple favorite students (or employees, or whatever) doesn't diminish that any one of them was another favorite.
2. I got better results when people believed I liked them.
3.   It's easy for people to believe I like them when I genuinely like them.
4. I got worse results when people thought I didn't like them.
5. I learned that I could *decide* to like people.
6. It's not that hard to like people.

And maybe more lessons. I'll have to think about that.

So, let's shift for a second. What is brown-nosing and why is it so disparaged? I think we tend to think of brown nosing as giving *excessive* favor to someone. Or trying *too hard* to please someone.

Those definitions seem to imply that brown-nosing is insincere. Fake. Having ulterior motives.

Suppose, instead, that you genuinely like someone. And you are kind to them because you want to be a kind person. Does that make you a brown-noser?

Pair up and discuss.

Ok. Time's up. I think no. I think that is simply being a kind, gentle, generous human being. The kind of human being that I aspire to be. I want to be kind because I want to be kind. I'm not going to let my boss (for illustration purposes only) being a jerk turn me into an unkind person.

That gives him (or her) WAY more power over my behavior

and life than I am willing to give. They don't deserve that much control over me. So I refuse to do it.

Now, keep in mind that I am a human, and an imperfect one, at that. (Just ask my wife. She has PLENTY of evidence.) So sometimes I'm not great at that. But I'm pretty good most of the time.
Remember the golden rule? "Do unto others…"? Yeah, that one. Then there's the "Platinum Rule" that became popular several years ago. "Treat others how THEY want to be treated."

I don't know what the right way to be is. Maybe it's being a chameleon (I prefer "chameleon" to "doormat." I don't think they're the same thing.) Let me explain.

When I was in high school, my dad told me that I was a chameleon. "When you learn what someone wants, you give it to them."

I call this superpower of mine "pushing buttons." Frankly, it's super fun to push buttons. I might mis-spell your name on purpose to get a reaction. No reaction? No fun pushing your buttons and I stop. But I digress.

On the flip side, when I learn that you love chocolate cake, I will probably share with you frequently. THAT's what I think my dad meant when he called me a chameleon. I discover what people want, and I give it to them.

This is powerful when you are dealing with your boss. I've heard it called the Fascination Factor. Whatever my boss is interested in is FASCINATING to me.

If I can be constantly depended on to give my boss what he or she wants or needs, I become more reliable in their eyes. I may get a little more flexibility. A little more grace. A little more consideration.

None of those things is bad. And maybe it can be enough of an adjustment in the interaction and relationship between us to make it just a little bit easier to work with the Boss from Hell.

CHAPTER THREE

MASTERING THE ART OF MIND
READING: PREDICTING EVER-
CHANGING EXPECTATIONS

"Don't ask questions you don't want the answer to." I have coached a lot of people on this.

"Well, I want to know the expectations."

Do you? Really?

If so, that's great. But make sure you do.

Communication is a funny thing. We all think we're amazing communicators. Super clear message, easy to understand, and impossible to misunderstand.

I had no idea how bad I was at communicating until I promoted to a leadership role. I gave simple instructions. Clear. Airtight. "Pick up these items from these places."

And somehow, the employee would find a way to screw it up. And not just a little. But to incredible degrees.

I once asked a ramp driver to bring two strings of orange dollies (each string has four dollies) to the gate we were working to offload freight from an airplane.

He brought TWO DOLLIES. That's it. I needed eight. He brought two. So, who was responsible for making this colossal failure?

Both of us.

I didn't clarify that I needed two strings—eight dollies. He thought he understood, so he didn't clarify, "Just two dollies? That's all you need?"

Both of us were wrong.

I once worked for a manager who, I believe, was intimidated by me. She would go days—I mean literal *days* without saying a word to me. And her office was across the hallway from my cube, so it wasn't like we didn't see each other.

We would pass each other in the hall, and she would give me a crooked smile and a nod. But no words. No "Hello," no "Good morning." Not even a "Happy Monday!"

In my youthful arrogance, I wanted to see how long until she would speak to me. I think it was over a month.

A MONTH! And she didn't say a word to me. NOTHING.

I finally asked her if we should be meeting on a regular basis so that I could make sure I was working on the right things. She decided that was a good idea, and things improved from there.

So, who was at fault that I went so long without any direction?

Both of us.

My point is that you can't read people's minds. Trust me. I've been married 33 years, and I *still* can't read my wife's mind. And to be fair, she's pretty crappy at reading mine.

I have spent a lot of time coaching people who have

struggled in their relationships. In every case, when I ask if the person has discussed the issue with their spouse, parent, child, boss, or whatever, the answer has always been "not yet."

What about bad bosses?

I hear a lot of things like "We do the same thing every day, so I shouldn't have to tell my people what to do every time."

And I wonder, "Why isn't that person doing what their leader thinks is expected?" The answer inevitably comes back to, "Oh, I didn't realize that's what they wanted me to do."

So, let me get this straight: You expect someone else to read your mind, and they think you should be reading your mind.

And you both suck at it.

Stop it! Stop trying to read people's minds and stop expecting them to be able to read yours.

Ask questions. Find out what is needed.

I get it. Asking questions *feels* like it's coming from weakness. You don't know something, so you have to ask.

But trust me: Asking questions is a strength. Especially if you have really good questions.

I have discovered that I'm pretty good at asking deep and meaningful questions. Maybe you're good at that, too.

When you're asked to change a procedure, produce a report, do something new…maybe you find a hole in the plan. Maybe there's a flaw. Something hasn't been considered.

Ask.

Maybe there are multiple priorities that all seem to have the same urgency and deadline. You probably can't do everything for everyone all the time. Which thing is most important?

Ask.

Or don't.

I know that seems counterintuitive. But trust me. Sometimes, asking is the way to go. Other times, *not* asking is best.

I've been the victim of changes in expectations from bosses. My normal go-to is to get them to clarify focus, intent, purpose, and priority.

Frankly, it's surprising how many times some of those things have never been considered. It's kind of fun to find the gaps that might result in some change—especially if the change is positive.

OR don't ask.

I can't tell you how many things I used to have to provide to my bosses on a regular basis, that I simply forgot about, and no one ever said anything about it, and now it's no longer a thing.

Some things are done only because "we've always done it." Maybe they're OK to suspend. Maybe no one needs the information that was being provided. Maybe a transition at higher levels has rendered that thing obsolete. And by asking about it, you might reignite interest in it.

So don't ask questions.

Confused? Don't be. Just read your boss's mind so you know what the priority is.

And when you can't read their mind, it's OK to ask questions. Just make sure to ask questions that you want answers to. Getting clear communication from your boss is your responsibility, and when you're good at it, it will help you navigate interacting with the Boss from Hell.

21

CHAPTER FOUR

NINJA TACTICS FOR SURVIVING MICROMANAGEMENT

22

First, let's address why bosses micromanage. I can think of a few reasons. If you come up with something different, let me know and I'll add it to this chapter.

Some bosses micromanage because it keeps them connected with the work that their team members are doing. They are concerned that if they lose touch with the functions or processes of their teams, they will lose connection with the end output.

Or when they were in the position they promoted from, their system worked for them, so they expect it to work for everyone else. I teased my wife when we were newly married that "There are two ways to do things. Your way and the wrong way." (The joke wasn't that funny to her, for anyone keeping score.) Some bosses believe their old way of doing things is still best—or that it should be the only way.

And some bosses micromanage because they don't have confidence in their team members' ability to get the job done. This can be an indication of an actual performance issue, but it's also a possible indication that the boss suffers from the fear of his image being damaged.

Three reasons. Maybe more. Let's take each of these individually, because how you deal with them will be slightly different.

I have had jobs that I truly enjoyed. When I promoted, my duties changed, and the tasks that I was skilled at were no longer my primary responsibility.

I dealt with this by hovering. By telling my leads how they should perform the functions. By stepping into the operation (instead of standing back to keep a larger perspective), the boss is trying to protect her image, because she imagines our screw-ups are a direct reflection of her capability.

The problem is that my strengths and weaknesses don't automatically become the strengths and weaknesses of my employees. They may have better ways of doing things.

The other problem that we tend to forget (as well as do our bosses) is that promoting from a job they were good at does not automagically make them good at managing the job they were promoted from.

I had a task that was highly visible. My team was being watched by the director and the vice president.

There was a lot of pressure, so I stepped in and told them how to perform the task. My way would save them time and resources.

And they blew it. I got an angry call from the director telling me how much my team sucked. And he was right. But it wasn't my team. They were running with MY plan.

My plan stunk. If I had let them do their thing, we probably would have been successful. But how do you do that when you're dealing with the Boss from Hell?

Second, when the boss has done the job you're now doing and was pretty successful, she might tell you how you should do it. This one can be a little bit tougher. The best thing I've seen is to listen to understand. What worked for the boss and why? Maybe their process is best—but remember that process and personality are different. Adopting processes is fantastic. Adopting personality is problematic.

I try to coach every new leader that I promote that I do NOT want them to be like me. The world really only needs one *me*. I want them to find and develop their own leadership style and become the best at being them.

This micromanager, however, is more focused on the individual steps than on the end result.

To deal with this micromanager, you both need to be clear on what the end result is—and on your ability to get the team there. Reassure the micromanaging leader that you have things under control. Maybe ask questions to clarify expectations.

I had one of these micromanagers who came into my operation and started nosing around. She was getting in the way. I then noticed that there was an urgent need to have something done away from the main functions of the team, and I asked my boss to do the task. It was a legitimate request. The thing needed to be done. And she was there, ready and available to do it.

It was later that I realized that giving her the simple assignment accomplished three tasks: Got her out of the way, reassured her that I had things under control, and accomplished the small task.

Win-win-win. And really, I was the ultimate winner, because

the micromanager started leaving me alone.

Finally, the micromanaging boss wants to make sure that things are done right and well. So, reassure them. And then get them out of the way.

Now, the third micromanager. The image-conscious manager. This is the person who doesn't like to be wrong or diminished in any way. Your failure equals their failure.

It's a faulty belief, but we're talking about what YOU can do to deal with the micromanaging leader—not fixing their bad beliefs.

First, don't diminish the image. Protect it. Maybe you ask their opinion. Second, let them be the person with the answers. Let them be the leader. Let them be the hero of their story. Don't take that from them.

I was newly promoted and my boss said something slightly incorrect about me. I corrected her instantly and publicly.

Bad move. I damaged (at least in her mind) her image.

Let them be right in public. Coach upwards and correct in private. Let them save face.

This micromanager will take some time to work with. They need to become assured that you won't be an embarrassment to them. Ask for support. Let them coach you. You might gain some valuable feedback on how to approach your job—or even insight into the micromanager's belief systems and priority lists, but even if you don't, you're investing in your future relationship. Teach the micromanager, over time, with results, that you can be trusted to protect their image. Then maybe, slowly, they stop being the Boss from Hell.

CHAPTER FIVE

DIPLOMATIC DEFIANCE: STANDING YOUR GROUND WITHOUT GETTING FIRED

During a general life coaching session I was conducting recently, a woman couldn't decide if she wanted to talk about money issues she was having—or maybe relationship problems she had with her in-laws. She vacillated between the two and finally landed on the money issues.

Her "money issue," as it turns out, wasn't a problem with not having enough, but it was a problem that she wasn't adding any money to the household income. She felt that somehow diminished her value or her role. During the session, I told her about another coaching session I had with another person on a totally unrelated topic, but I made the same comment to her that I had made in the earlier session: Does everything come down to personal self-worth or self-value?

She pondered for a minute, and the more she thought about it, the more she realized that her mind was blown.

It all starts with your own self-image/self-worth. Call it what you want—it's the same thing.

Here's another thing that you are going to have to trust me on. You (yes, YOU) have infinite value and worth ***simply because you are here.*** You don't have to earn it. And certainly, no one has to agree. And it is true.

Of course, that is also true for me, and for the Boss, and for everyone else on the planet.

Let that sink in for a minute. IF you understand that you have infinite worth and value simply because you are here, what does that change?

For the woman I was coaching, it meant that the dollar amount she contributed (or didn't contribute) to the household income was meaningless. Her contribution was herself. Her presence. Her existence. She was raising several kids. She helped support her husband in his career, and in his schooling before that.

Your value doesn't come from your job title. It doesn't come from your annual income. It doesn't come from any awards or degrees you have earned. It comes from you. Your existence.

Now, suppose your boss treats you as if you are less valuable than you know you are.

Two questions: First, what does that mean about you? Take a minute to think about this, but I'll tell you the answer. It means NOTHING about you.

Absolutely nothing. Not a single thing.

You may have seen videos online from people who are masters in their craft in common settings. I remember one where expert violinist Joshua Bell was in the subway station playing for spare change. He did this just for fun. Just to see what would happen. Over a thousand people walked by, but only 27 people gave him money. Now, when he plays in concert halls, he can command hundreds of dollars *per person* in ticket prices.

But in the subway, people walked by, not even noticing. What changed Joshua's value/talent/skill from the subway to Carnegie Hall?

Nothing. Except the subway audience didn't recognize his greatness (except one person, who tipped him well). The concertgoers DO recognize his amazing talent, and they pay well to listen to it.

Now, it is entirely possible that your boss doesn't recognize or respect or honor your infinite worth. That's something you don't have any control over.

But that leads us to question two: What does your boss's misunderstanding about you and your worth mean *about you?*

Again, the answer is NOTHING.

If the Boss can't (or doesn't, or won't) recognize your value and worth, that doesn't change your worth.

Those subway patrons who didn't recognize Joshua Bell just didn't recognize his greatness. Doesn't mean he's not great. Just mean they didn't recognize it.

If the boss treats you unkindly, that's a conversation we will have in chapter 10, so hold on. But for now, it's important for you to recognize your infinite worth.

I need you to be sold on YOU.

Then, we can discuss diplomatic defiance. Being defiant needs to include three things:

1. Respect. Defiance without respect for the boss's position (even if not for the person himself or

herself) is required. Disrespect, in my opinion, is never justified. You can disagree without being disagreeable. It is never acceptable to be disrespectful. It might be best to use language and be in a situation where you can help the boss protect his or her image, as we have discussed previously.

2. Communication. You will need to clearly explain what the problem is. Make sure your argument makes sense and is justified. Be logical and thoughtful. Maybe you've discovered that adding a specific data point to a required report will triple the time required to gather the information. Explain that. Be clear and concise. Leave emotions at the door. Ask about priorities. (If I do this the way you want, I won't be able to do the other thing you've asked me to do. Which is more important?)

3. Confidence. Think of your boss as an ally. The two of you are working together to solve a problem, and because you are closer to the action, you have a better understanding of what is required.

The job is the job. You may not be able to change required tasks, but it is entirely possible that someone who isn't in the thick of it, like you are, has made decision that affect your ability to do what is needed.

There have been a few times that I have stood up for myself in a public setting. It's not always the best way to do things because you run the risk of creating a showdown between you and your boss.

And your boss wants to win. So, keep the showdowns to a minimum. But if it has to happen, find a friend.

Use a trusted peer as a sounding board. Make sure you are justified in taking the steps you are proposing. And have them as backup when you make the public showdown happen.

This can go badly, so use it as a last resort. Give the boss an out, if necessary. Maybe you (or you and the friend) speak to the boss in a more private setting.

Remember…the boss is people, too. You don't want to be publicly flogged—neither does he. You don't want to be called on the carpet—don't do it to her.

Be kind and respectful to the boss—and to *you*. And you just might be able to survive the Boss from Hell.

CHAPTER SIX

THE ART OF "YES, BOSS":
NAVIGATING THE PERILS OF
CONSTANT AGREEMENT

People pleasing happens when we try to manipulate someone by being agreeable to every request made. This can become problematic in every relationship, and certainly in the boss/employee dynamic. At work, sometimes we call the people pleaser a "Yes-man" or "Yes-woman."

However, we have jobs with bosses who have the expectation that we will perform according to the tasks that the job requires. How, then, can we distinguish between being a "Yes, Boss" People Pleaser (which I will now just call a "Yes, Boss" and a fully functioning employee?

The short answer is "It depends."

And that is pretty much because I'm dodging making a full commitment to an answer in print, but give me a chance to explain myself.

In most relationships, the most reliable way to distinguish between being kind and helpful and being a people pleaser is to consider motivations and desires. *Why* are you agreeing to do something? Are you trying to manipulate the person (this includes trying to make them happy, or upset, or anything else; or to trying to keep them from getting angry or frustrated; or to get any other resultant behavior)

Sometimes, however, doing what the boss asks is just part of the job.

So, suppose my boss asks me to stay late so that I can get a report done. I really don't want to, and the report isn't part of my normal duties. If I want the boss to lay off me for a few days and I accept the assignment hoping that she will give me some grace, maybe that's people pleasing. However, if I want the boss to know that I am reliable, competent, and worthy of getting promoted, maybe that's not.

It gets confusing because from the outside, the end result of me staying late to get the report done looks the same to my wife, to my peers, and to my employees.

So, am I a "Yes, Boss" or an ambitious go-getter?

My critics will say I'm a "Yes, Boss." My supporters will say I'm ambitious. My question for you is, "Why does it matter?"

The answer to *that* question is nuanced, as well. First, why should I care what my critics think? They obviously don't think I'm as amazing as my wife thinks I am, so who cares? There is no vote, and it's not a democracy.

So, the real answer, as far as I am concerned, is for you, the kind reader of this ridiculously helpful book, to decide for yourself. Not for me, or for your boss, or for anyone else. What is the answer for you? And do you believe and like the reasons you are telling yourself?

And, making this issue even more sticky is the boss is dealing with his or her own "Yes, Boss"-ness. When the Boss agrees to take on extra tasks (which then get passed on to you!), did they do that because of their own aspirations, or are they trying to control something about their own boss? And just like for the rest of us, the answer can be confusing, because I may not know the whole context of the assignment when my share is handed down to me. Maybe the boss volunteered to take on extra tasks because it will look good on their resume, or maybe they love leading the task force, or they want to be involved in a certain emerging aspect of the company's growth. And when *my* workload changes because the boss needs *my* support to contribute the way that he wants to, there's no flashing sign that labels the boss as a "Yes, Boss" or "Ambitions Go-getter"

I lead the safety team in my current job. Is that a "Yes, Boss" move? Not really. I could push that onto someone else's plate, but I have a few good (I think, anyway) reasons for keeping that assignment. And during a recent meeting, the question was raised about how members of the team should deal with safety infractions that they encounter.

My answer: "I want you to get it right for yourselves, first. I want you to be 100% safe. I want you to take care of you before you start worrying about how everyone else is doing." That's how I feel and what I told them. I don't need someone telling me how much another person is breaking the rules if you can't follow them yourself.

I feel the same way (not that you asked me, but you *are* reading my book, so you are going to get my opinion. You're welcome) about the "Yes, Boss" issue.

Get clear about yourself for yourself. If you are solid on how you feel about what your motivation is who cares what anyone else thinks. In fact, trying to take on—or not take on—assignments or requests hoping that other people will think a specific way about you is *exactly* the wrong reason to do something. That's manipulative, and it's not successful. Because you can't control what anyone else thinks, anyways.

So, stop trying.

The boss asks you to do something extra. If it is really part of the job, then the answer is you should probably do it. Nothing wrong with pushing back and asking questions first, though. (Have we talked about that yet?) Make sure you are clear on what is being asked of you. Why is it needed? Who is using it and what for? That may adjust your approach, the priority you give to it, and your commitment to it.

But, if it's clear that the request is negotiable (sometimes, the boss is kind enough to tell you that "you can say no"), what is your reason for saying yes? If the reason isn't great, you have my permission to turn it down. Guilt-free.

The bottom line is that being a "Yes, Boss" only exists in other people's minds, and as long as you get centered on yourself, your job, your priorities, and your tasks, it doesn't matter what they think. Get the job done and go home.

And doing things because you want to do them (instead of trying to manipulate other people's opinions or experiences of you) is far less exhausting, which gives you more energy to deal with the Boss from Hell.

CHAPTER SEVEN

THE FINE ART OF STRATEGIC COMPLAINING: VENTING WITHOUT GETTING LABELED A WHINER

42

Not only is complaining cathartic, it's important in nudging the Boss from Hell to becoming a more manageable part of your workday. After all, how else can you share your concerns, thoughts, insights, and wisdom?

A rule I ask my employees to follow is to "complain upward." I want to hear their concerns. I can't fix a problem if I don't know it exists. I'd rather have them tell *me* what's on their mind than have them create a toxic workgroup by encouraging an environment where individual frustrations gain momentum and spiral into an uncontrollable mess.

I also want my boss to allow me to complain upward. This gives me a chance to vent about whatever is on my mind. Sometimes, believe it or not, I get frustrated with people, and I need to let it all out before I explode.

Now, it's fair to say that "complaining upward" isn't always successful. I called a boss one time to tell her about problems I was having in the operation. She started brainstorming solutions. That wasn't what I was looking for or even needed at the time.

Another time, the boss started defending himself, explaining why things were the way that they were. That, by the way, was a recipe for feeling unheard and unappreciated.

Another time, my boss told me I was wrong. Not that my thoughts and ideas were wrong, but that I was wrong for feeling the way that I was feeling. Not the way to garner trust, loyalty, and respect.

Communication with other people is always a little risky because we're so lousy at it. I remember a college Communications class that demonstrated how horrible we are at communicating by way of a drawing. I won't recreate it here, but imagine a drawing of a person on the left side of the page (she is the sender of the message) and a person on the right, who is the receiver. In the middle is the message.

The drawing demonstrated that there is a problem: between each person and the message is that person's total life experience. In the illustration, that summary of experiences was represented as a cloud. We have the summary of our life that, frankly, clouds our messages. Everything that we say and hear goes through a filter of our life experiences. The message can get convoluted. The good news is that it happens just all the time.

For example, when I tell you to put the ice cream scoop away, you imagine you know what I mean, because you keep your ice cream scoop in the drawer with the utensils. Or you may assume that because my ice cream scoop has been stored in the same drawer for hundreds of years, you know where it belongs. But what I didn't think to mention is that I've been thinking that it makes more sense that the ice cream scoop be stored with the spoons (which you use to eat ice cream) instead of with the random utensils.

Ensuring that an accurate message is both sent and received takes time, humility, and patience. Imagine the Boss telling you that you need to send a recap of why something went wrong with your team's performance. The Boss knows exactly what information is required, and she probably assumes that you do, too. After all, how hard is it to write a recap?

Really hard, it turns out, if you don't know what the recap is supposed to cover, who the intended audience is (my recap to my boss will look VERY different than a recap to the Vice President).

Problems with communications aside, it's still a necessary part of interacting with others. And when things at work get frustrating, you may need to talk about it. With the boss.

It is often safe to assume that having a complaint session with the boss will leave you feeling better, but it's important to take control of that meeting. Set expectations. Don't just dump on the boss. Understand what you are hoping to gain by meeting. You can increase your success exponentially if you preface your conversation with a summary of your expectations.

I'll give you some examples that you can try on:

1. Prepare the boss before starting the conversation. Open with a warning. Something like, "I am complaining upward." You might even ask permission to speak freely. Do you need the conversation to be off the record? Ask.
2. Set the expectation at the front end of the conversation that you are sharing information instead of looking for solutions. You can take some of the pressure off the boss (or at least shift it) by making it clear that you aren't asking for them to fix anything right now.
3. Of course, another popular option is to come to the meeting with solutions to any problem that you discuss.
4. Be aware of your tone. You are a competent

professional with concerns. Present yourself as a rational human sharing facts. Leave the drama at the door. Superfluous adjectives—especially if they bring up emotion—may not contribute to your cause. Stick to objective details.

5. Tell the boss that you need some time. It may make sense to schedule a meeting when the two of you can devote your full attention to the situation.

Of course, this list is not comprehensive, but hopefully it helps get you started. And if you sense that the tone of the meeting is not contributing to what you hope to accomplish, call it out.

Remind the boss that you aren't looking for solutions. Or that you just need to get something off your chest, and you need her to just be aware of where you're coming from. Or that as the boss, he probably should be aware of some things. Or that there is a work decision she needs to make so that you can get on with your life.

And maybe you need one of these meetings so that you can share some feedback about the conflict you are feeling with the boss. I remember the uncomfortable moment during an interview when I was asked to describe how I dealt with a personal conflict at work…and the person I had the conflict with was doing the interview. (I didn't get the job.)

Be kind, but objective. Share your concerns.

Interpersonal relationships are tough enough. Make things as simple as you can for both of you by identifying and setting expectations for the meeting. As you strengthen your communication skills, working with the Boss from Hell gets just a little bit easier.

CHAPTER EIGHT

COPING WITH CONSTANT CHANGE:
EMBRACING WHIPLASH

For some reason, we seem to have the impression that we are actually supposed to enjoy life. There is a belief among many people (at least the ones that I know) that we are somehow supposed to have joy in our lives. That ease, comfort, and a positive trend is somehow what should be expected.

Maybe it's that line from the Declaration of Independence that has tricked us into thinking that we should somehow have an easy existence.

I am not arguing that we should *not* have "life, liberty, and the pursuit of happiness," but I think we sometimes tend to forget that the unalienable right is the *pursuit* of happiness—not the *result* of happiness.

And this isn't a high-school Government class essay. I stopped writing those a LONG time ago, and I'm not really interested in proving my ignorance. But I think this is important to hash out for a few minutes.

I was listening to a podcast a while back. David Neagle hosts the "Successful Mind" podcast. Absolutely worth a listen. He was talking about the way people approach their jobs. The quote he said, at least the way I wrote it down, was: "It's not your job's responsibility to make you happy."

So, who (or what) has the responsibility to make us happy?

That's a question worthy of a lengthy discussion, and that's not really the purpose of this book. I'll just tell you what I think.

I don't know.

But I do know, for a certainty, that it's not your *job*. Or your boss. And if that's the case, it also means that it's not your boss's responsibility to make your job suck.

I have found that I can do that all by myself.

In my corporate experience, I have worked for several companies. Their names don't matter, and the industries could be anything. One thing that I experienced might surprise you (but maybe not) was that almost *all* of them had some level of corporate cultural humor poking fun at how rapidly change takes place. In fact, one company I worked for had an acronym touting how quickly we could expect change.

As I sit in an economy-class airplane seat, probably over somewhere in Kansas as I am writing this particular chapter, it is the year 2023. The things that I have seen transform the world over the years are astounding. I remember, for example, the first time I connected a computer to the Internet. I remember the awe I felt when I made my first call from a cordless phone.

I mean, really. Being able to talk to someone on the phone without the handset being connected to the wall via a curly cord was magical.

And technology is changing at breakneck speed, but I don't have to tell you that. And if I do, we have other problems.

In any case, my point is that *everything* is changing. And it's changing fast. So fast that it is getting impossible to keep up.

I learned an important lesson not that long ago. A podcast (yes, another one. I listen a lot to podcasts. Not a lot of podcasts—I don't have time for that. But I do listen a lot to podcasts. They can be pretty insightful. You should listen to mine if you haven't. Have I mentioned that yet? It's called Un-toxic Positivity—the Bad Boss Podcast. At least, I'm having a little fun with it.)

Anyways—I feel like I got a little sidetracked. Where was I?

Oh, yes. The lesson I learned on the podcast was that if you argue with reality, you will lose. But just every time.

Reality, (you know, what people are referring to when they say "it is what it is") is what is going on around us. It is the constant flood of changes in everything. Media, technology, the food pyramid, and even our jobs. And it's not going to slow down.

Frankly, it *can't* slow down. Businesses have to change, or they will die.

Remember Blockbuster Video? No? Well, that's exactly my point. A little company called Netflix started mailing DVDs to people. Movies came to you…you don't have to go to get them. Blockbuster didn't change their model fast enough, so as of right now, according to an article that I think I read a while back, there is exactly one Blockbuster video store left in the world.

Google it. I'm probably right.

My point is that change is going to happen. Jobs will change. The players in the jobs will change. Your boss will change.

The industry will change. Your relationships will change.

My best advice is to stop resisting the change. Accept it.

It doesn't matter how much you like it or hate it. Your opinion isn't going to stop *anything* from becoming different.

So how do you embrace the whiplash of constant change?

I don't know what will work for you, so I'll share what has worked for me:

1. Hate the change. Complain to your wife, husband, co-worker, boss, friend, mother, father, child, or grocery store cashier about how stupid the change is. Let them know that no one asked you about how to make a *better* change, and so now you have to deal with a *worse* change.
2. Hate how your life is different with the change. (The less time you spend here, the better.)
3. Open your mind to the possibility that the changed policy, management style, pricing, or whatever else is different might actually not be the worst thing you have ever experienced in your life.
4. Accept that this is the "new normal."
5. Completely forget how the old way was and realize that you have completely adopted the change.

Now, to be fair, I'm not always good at this. Sometimes this process goes pretty quickly, but sometimes it takes a while. The whole process, however, is important. Grieve the old. That is OK, and probably healthy. (At least that's what I imagine my therapist friend would say if I actually asked her. I'm pretty sure I'm right on this one.)

Change has to happen. Don't blame the boss, even if the boss is the one who came up with the bright idea to do things differently. And of course, not all change is positive or productive. Some changes need to be un-changed or re-changed.

Step up and be a part of that process. Share your wisdom and insight. Make sure the decision makers are aware of how their decisions impact aspects of the operation that they certainly didn't consider when they considered making changes.

But in any case, when change is out of your control and it happens, accept it, because anything else is going to make life more miserable than is necessary.

And hopefully, you won't blame everything on the Boss from Hell.

54

CHAPTER NINE

DEALING WITH UNREALISTIC EXPECTATIONS: WHEN YOUR BOSS THINKS YOU HAVE SUPERPOWERS

56

You have something that you don't realize you have, and once I uncover it for you, you will be simultaneously relieved and a little bit confused.

You have an instruction manual for your boss.

Maybe you have wished you had an instruction manual so that you could figure out what they want, or what makes them tick. That's not the kind of instruction manual you have. No, you have the one that tells you what your boss *should* want, or what *should* make them tick.

We all have manuals for everyone in every relationship we have. A book (it doesn't really exist in print form, if you were wondering about that) that we imagine exists that outlines how other people should behave. What they should say or do in a situation. When we become frustrated with another person, it's because they aren't following the manual we have for that person.

Let me give you a few non-work examples.

My 16-year-old son has the regular task of taking the trash can out to the street. This should happen every Sunday because trash day is Monday. He has heard this about a million times from me, from my wife, and from me again. I can't imagine that a world exists where he doesn't understand his weekly duty.

Yet, every Sunday night, we remind him that the trash needs to go out. And every Sunday night, he resists. And every Sunday night, I (or my wife—or both) get frustrated because this scenario played out AGAIN.

My instruction manual for my son says that he should notice that the calendar indicates that the day is Sunday, and that it is dark outside, indicating evening. He should also notice that the trash can hasn't yet been taken to the street, so he should happily and proactively make the 50-foot trek from the garage to the street.

Guess what? He hasn't read my manual. So, irregardless (yes, I used that word. It's a tribute to my mother-in-law, and I stand by it) of how many times I remind him, or of how frustrated I get, or how loudly I ask, he still hasn't read my manual for him.

And even if he had, it doesn't mean he's going to follow my manual for him.

Remember? We can't control other people's actions. As much as we think we should be able to, it just doesn't work that way.

The other crazy thing? I've never told him what my manual says about him. Somehow, I imagine he should just *know* what my expectations are.

If you have a boss who thinks you're a superhero and therefore has unrealistic expectations of you, I can pretty safely assume that you haven't had that conversation. I have coached a LOT of people with manuals that aren't being followed by people in their lives, and NOT ONCE have I coached someone who had talked with the person about it.

So, we make a lot of assumptions.

I get it. It can be awkward. It might be uncomfortable. Unfortunately, that awkwardness and discomfort is the currency you must pay to have a better relationship.

We're talking bosses, but we're also talking every other relationship. Peers. Subordinates. Spouse. Children. Parents. In-laws. Friends. All of them.

The simple thing is to complain about how the other person is unreasonable. Or that they have unrealistic expectations.

The best thing, however, is to have a conversation. If the boss has unrealistic expectations of you, do they know it? If they did, what might change? What's the worst case that might happen? More work? Maybe, but probably not. Help? Maybe. That wouldn't be all that awful, would it? A release from some of the demands? Maybe. Also, wouldn't be too bad. No change? So, you're in the same boat you're already in.

Spend a few minutes to discover what you have on your boss's manual. What are you expecting? What do you need from him or her? Communicate that.

Then, at the same time, ask what is on their manual for you. You might ask questions like:

- Help me understand what you are hoping I accomplish?
- What are your expectations for this project?
- How much time should I anticipate spending on this?
- If I can't meet your deadline or other expectations, how would you like me to proceed?

An open dialogue might be the starting point for better

understanding. You understanding the boss can't be all that bad, and the boss better understanding you, your skill set, your competencies, and your interests can't hurt too much, either.

And maybe, just maybe, you'll have a better chance of working with (not just for) the Boss from Hell.

CHAPTER TEN

BOUNDARIES: BOSS OR BFF?

62

Boundaries are easily misunderstood. They are catching a lot of attention these days, and I think that they're critical for surviving almost any relationship. Unfortunately, for many of us, we assume that having boundaries is an "ethical" way to control peoples' behavior. "I have a boundary that you won't ask me to do anything I don't want to do."

Nope. We don't the option (or the ability!) to control other people. Heck. We have enough trouble trying to control ourselves.

Think of a boundary as the front door to your house. It's just there, minding its own business. In fact, most of the world doesn't even know where it is or even that it exists—though they probably assume that, at least in theory, it exists. The purpose of having a front door isn't for everyone to know that you have a front door—or even where your front door is. The *real* purpose is to protect you.

Your front door protects you from animals, from weather, and from intruders. If you don't share the key, it can protect you from your in-laws, as well—but that's another book.

When a person comes to your house, the door keeps the curiosity-seeker from wandering through your kitchen and rifling through your junk drawer. After all, it's none of their business how many pairs of scissors you have to keep in there because your kids keep taking them and never putting them back away where they belong so that when you need them you can't find them so you go and buy another scissor and then when you tidy up the house you find eleven scissors and you put them all back in the junk drawer where they belong and then you yell at your kids that it's OK that they borrow the scissors, but PUT THEM BACK IN THE JUNK DRAWER WHEN YOU ARE DONE WITH THEM SO I DON'T HAVE TO SPEND MY ENTIRE PAYCHECK REPLACING SCISSORS THAT YOU HAVE HIDDEN IN YOUR ROOM!

Not based on real events.

The boundary lets the world know that "behind this door is a safe space, and you are only allowed if you are invited."

So, there you go. That's your boundary. It is something *you* decide to protect *you*. It is not something that you decide to change or fix someone else.

Let's consider some scenarios.

I'm not sure if you noticed but for the last couple of years, we have had a global pandemic. At the risk of losing some of you because you think I'm going to make this a political thing, let me share a few things that I observed.

I know an older couple who were very concerned with their health. Both were cancer survivors. Both were old enough to be classified as "high risk." They were concerned about exposure to the virus. So, they established a boundary that no one who does not live in their home is allowed to enter the home.

But what about me? I'm a decent guy. I wash my hands at

least twice a day. I brush my teeth, and I shower almost weekly. But I don't live there. You're saying I can't come in and have a chat with MY FAMILY?

That is exactly what I am saying.

To be clear, their boundary wasn't that I couldn't visit. I did visit. Many times. I just stood outside their home and talked to them through the window that was cracked enough that we could hear each other.

The boundary wasn't there to control my behavior. It was there to protect them. They kept their front door closed to people who didn't live there. Including me.

Now, let's consider another pandemic story. Also based on real events that I heard about somewhere on the Internet.

Suppose you have a school that requires students to wear masks, and you personally don't think the mask mandate is right, or valid, or necessary, or whatever else. Can you set a boundary that your kids don't have to wear a mask?

Careful…this can get tricky. You can have a personal rule that you don't wear masks. Cool on you. BUT you don't get to "enforce" your boundary by requiring the school, or the store, or the workplace to let you roam around unmasked.

See how that works? The older couple set a boundary that no one gets to enter their home unless it is their own address. The school gets to set a boundary that no student gets to come into the classroom without a mask. You don't, however, get to set a boundary that the school HAS to allow little Penelope to play with her friends.

Make sense? Your boundary protects you. (If you do this to me, I will do this to protect myself). Your boundary *can not* attempt to control someone else. (I am worth $40,000,000 dollars, so you *will* pay my requested wage.)

See the difference?

Now, let's talk bosses.

It is absolutely appropriate to have boundaries at work. But don't confuse a boss trying to get the job done with crossing your boundaries.

Have you ever tried to write a job description? It's crazy hard. Don't believe me? Try to summarize your current job in a couple of paragraphs. Don't forget to include *every possible thing* that you might be ever asked to do ever in the course of your employment.

It's not really possible. Which means you might be asked to do things that aren't specifically documented as a part of your job. Just like the Ten Commandments don't really cover EVERY POSSIBLE SIN. Just the big ones.

So, when the Boss from Hell asks you to do something, it's important to understand whether it's part of the job or not.

If it's not, please, have a boundary. If it is, you should just understand that it is part of the job. Jobs aren't supposed to be fun all the time. Sometimes there are sucky parts that no one likes. Sorry to break that to you.

A lot of times, boundaries have to do with *treatment*. Suppose your boss calls you "Shorty." It's totally fine to not like that. So, your boundary might look like, "If you call me 'Shorty,' I will not respond. My name is Denise Jr.'"

Profanity might ignite another boundary. Washing his car or picking up her dry cleaning (unless you are a Personal

Assistant) might invoke boundaries.

Another cool thing about boundaries is that you don't necessarily have to tell the person that they are approaching—or have crossed—a boundary. Remove yourself from the situation. Simply and quietly. In some cases, it may be important to notify the person that they are approaching or have crossed a boundary.

Expect some resistance. People don't like finding out that they have crossed a boundary. They might become upset. Remember that they are upset with the boundary. And that doesn't mean that there's anything wrong with the boundary...or with you.

What about when the boss wants to be besties?

I have been invited to socialize with my team members. I have a boundary that I don't do that. (I can't imagine anyone wanting to spend more time with me than is absolutely necessary, to be fair.)

I have been invited to socialize with former bosses. Sometimes I go, sometimes I don't go. When I go, I go on purpose. I go because I want to. When I don't go, I don't explain or justify. I just politely decline.

Sometimes it will be necessary to explain your boundaries, but not always. Just notice that they are there. Make sure you are clear on what they are and why you have them. Remember that they protect *you*, but they do not control others. And protect yourself from the Boss from Hell

ABOUT THE AUTHOR

Ken Williams is a certified life coach with an advanced certification in faith-based coaching. His specialty and purpose in life is to help people survive difficult bosses. His "Bad Boss Podcast" shares the insights that have worked for him and for his coaching clients and can be found on any podcast platform.

In addition to being the author of <u>Surviving the Boss from Hell,</u> he has written <u>How to Manager: Skills and Tactics to Become Slightly Above Average.</u> He is also the author of the Amazon best-selling business books <u>21 Days to Success through Networking</u> and <u>21 Days to Success with LinkedIn,</u> the less-than-helpful grammar book, <u>Irregardless,</u> and his favorite literary classic, <u>The Chocolate Cake Phenomenon—A More Delicious Way to Minister.</u> You should buy them all.

You can reach out to him at ken@kenwilliamscoaching, or schedule time to meet with him at https://tidycal.com/kenwilliams/intro-meeting